DK

A Dorling Kindersley Book

Text Terry Martin
Project Editor Caroline Bingham
US Editor Camela Decaire
Senior Art Editor Sarah Wright-Smith
Deputy Managing Editor Mary Ling
Production Louise Barratt
Medical Consultant Dr. Thomas Kramer
MBBS, MRCS, LRCP
Picture Researcher Lorna Ainger
Additional photography by Paul Bricknell,
Philip Dowell, R.K. Emp, Jo Foord,
Barnabas Kindersley, Dave King, Ian O'Leary,
Susanna Price, Tim Ridley, Steve Shott.

Published in Canada in 1996
by Scholastic Canada Ltd.,
123 Newkirk Road,
Richmond Hill, Ontario L4C 3G5

First published in Great Britain in 1996
by Dorling Kindersley Limited,
9 Henrietta Street, London WC2E 8PS

Copyright © 1996 Dorling Kindersley Limited

Canadian Cataloguing in Publication Data

Martin, Terry, 1971–
Why do we laugh? : questions children ask about the human body

(Why books)
ISBN 0-590-24955-X

1. Human physiology – Juvenile literature. I. Title.
II. Series: Martin, Terry, 1971–   . Why books.

QP37. M3 1996   j612   C96-931005-6
Color reproduction by Chromagraphics,
Singapore
Printed and bound in Italy by L.E.G.O.

The publisher would like to thank the
following for their kind permission
to reproduce their photographs:
t top, b bottom, l left, r right, c center FC front cover
The Image Bank: Blue Lemon (Why do I have to go...?: c), Romilly Lockyer: endpapers;
Tony Stone Images: Lori Adamski Peek (Why does my heart...?: c), Peter Cade (Why should
I wear...?: c), Bruce Forster (Why do I lose...?: br), Andy Sacks (Why do I have eyelashes?: br).

Questions

Why do we laugh?

Why do I get hungry?

Why do I lose my
baby teeth?

Why should I wear
sunscreen?

Why do I have eyelashes?

Why does my heart beat
faster when I run?

Why are there twins?

Why do I have to go to bed?

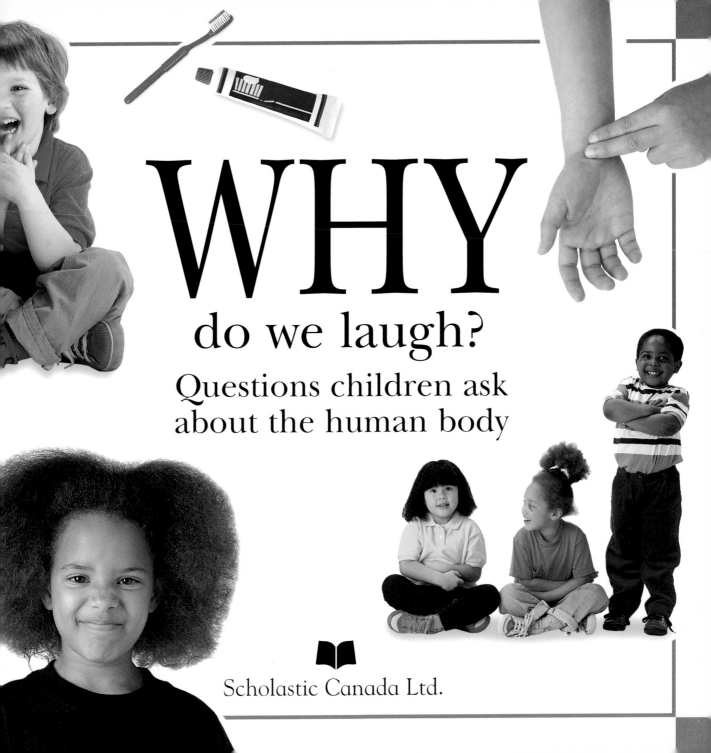

WHY

do we laugh?

Questions children ask
about the human body

Scholastic Canada Ltd.

Why do we laugh?

Laughter is one way of releasing tension when you find something funny. Your face muscles lift up the corners of your lips, and

Why do I cry?
A good long cry is another way to release tension. A tear gland in each eye produces water as soon as your brain sends the message to cry. Tears also help wash dust or eyelashes out of your eyes.

your breathing muscle, or diaphragm, pushes air through your voice box.

Why am I ticklish?
Your body has lots of sensitive spots. When they are touched lightly, your brain makes you react quickly, but since it doesn't hurt, you laugh!

Why do I

Food is very important, and feeling hungry is your body's way of telling you that you need to eat. Food gives your body the energy to work properly and to help you grow.

Why am I thirsty?
Your body contains water, which you lose by sweating and going to the bathroom. Feeling thirsty is your brain's way of saying that it's time to replace this lost water.

get hungry?

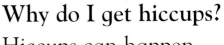

Why does my tummy grumble?
Growls and gurgles from your tummy
can sound funny. They happen when
your tummy is empty of food and
its muscles are churning
around the gas and
juices left inside.

Why do I get hiccups?
Hiccups can happen
if you eat or drink too
quickly. They are
short, sudden gasps
of air, caused
when your
diaphragm
moves up and
down more sharply
than usual.

Why do I lose my

You have to lose your baby, or milk, teeth to make room for an adult set. Children have only 20 teeth. Most grown-ups have 32!

Why are my teeth different shapes?
Teeth are designed to help you eat. You have biters at the front, sharp tearers at the sides, and flat chewers,

baby teeth?

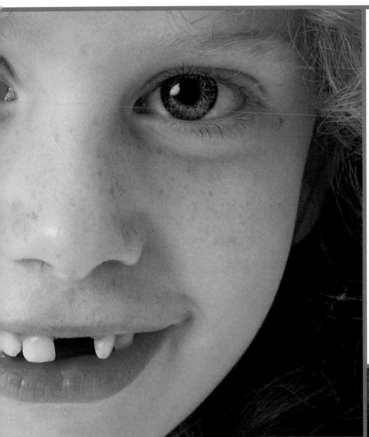

Why do I have to brush my teeth?
Millions of tiny germs live in your mouth, feeding on food stuck between your teeth. Unless you brush well, these germs will make your smile disappear – tooth by tooth.

or molars, at the back. Animals grow special teeth, too. Lions have long fangs to tear meat, while cows have lots of molars to munch grass.

The sun gives off harmful ultraviolet rays that can cause your skin to burn – and that hurts! Sunscreen stops these rays from reaching your skin.

Why do I have freckles?
You have a dark brown coloring called melanin in your skin. Freckles appear where there are patches of melanin.

wear sunscreen?

Why do people have different-colored skin?

A person's skin color depends on how much melanin there is in the top layer of their skin, the epidermis. The more melanin, the darker the skin color. If your skin has a yellow tint, you have a coloring called carotene.

Why do I have eyelashes?

Two hundred eyelashes help protect each of your eyes. If they are touched – even by a bit of lint – these super-sensitive hairs "tell" your eyelids to close instantly.

Why doesn't it hurt when my hair is cut?
Healthy hair is nothing more than dead cells. You won't feel any pain when these dead cells are cut, but it would hurt to pull them out from the living root!

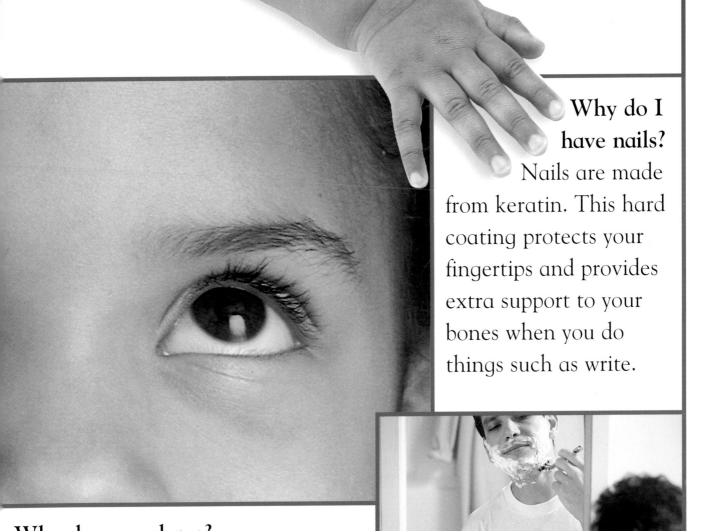

Why do I have nails?

Nails are made from keratin. This hard coating protects your fingertips and provides extra support to your bones when you do things such as write.

Why do men shave?

Men's bodies produce a chemical that makes body hair grow. Men shave to stop beards from growing.

Why does my heart beat

"Wait for me!" When you run or exercise, your heart beats faster than normal to rush oxygen-rich blood to your hard-working muscles, where it is used to make energy.

Why do I blush?

Just under your skin's surface are tiny blood vessels. When you are embarrassed, these vessels widen, so more blood flows through them, making your face red.

faster when I run?

Why do I have veins?
Your heart pumps blood to every far corner of your body. Veins return blood to the heart for fresh supplies of oxygen.

Why do headstands turn my face red?
You're not built to walk around on your head, so your heart has a hard time keeping blood away from it when you're upside down!

Why are there twins?

No, you're not seeing double! A baby grows from a fertilized egg. Identical twins are born when this egg splits into two parts.

Why do people have different-colored eyes?

In giving you life, your parents passed on a special mixture of chemicals called genes, which determined the way you look – including your eye color.

Why is my hair curly?

Human heads are like giant pincushions, full of tiny holes, or follicles, from which hairs grow. Round follicles produce straight hair. Curly hairs come from flat follicles.

Everybody needs a good night's sleep. It's when your brain sorts out the things that happen each day, and when your body has a chance to heal itself.

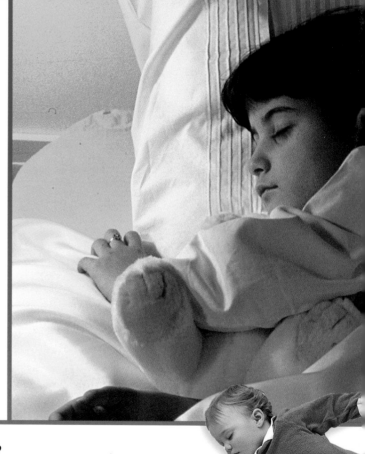

Why do babies sleep so much?

Newborn babies will happily sleep for 20 hours a day (with lots of waking up in between!). They need plenty of sleep because they have a lot of growing to do.

go to bed?

Why does a stretch feel good?

Muscles get shorter and fatter when they are working. It feels good to stretch them out, and it helps you relax.

Why do I yawn?

Open wide! You take a big, deep gulp of air whenever your body needs more oxygen to help you "wake up."